Take
Good
Care

Taking good care of yourself is beautiful, challenging, life-changing work. It's about learning how to hear your own voice. How to recognize your own truth. How to advocate for the things you need—with tenderness, and with fierceness too.

And as you begin to prioritize your well-being, and strengthen your boundaries, things change. You trust yourself. You spend your energy differently. Your days look new. And so do your possibilities.

When you take good care of yourself, you end up with more. More strength. More authenticity. More of the things you want to do. More of the things that light you up. More energy. *More you.*

Care for your
well-being

WHO WAS I BEFORE I BECAME WHO THE WORLD TOLD ME TO BE?

Glennon Doyle

When you look back at yourself as a young child, what strikes you? There can be an incredible sense of affirmation in rediscovering who you were, innately, before the world shifted and shaped you—and in accessing those elements of your being that are deep and old and true.

What are three surprising, remarkable, or noteworthy characteristics you remember about yourself?

Reading a favorite childhood book, eating a favorite childhood food, dancing the way your young self used to... what is a small but symbolic way you can rekindle the presence of each of these characteristics in your own life, right now?

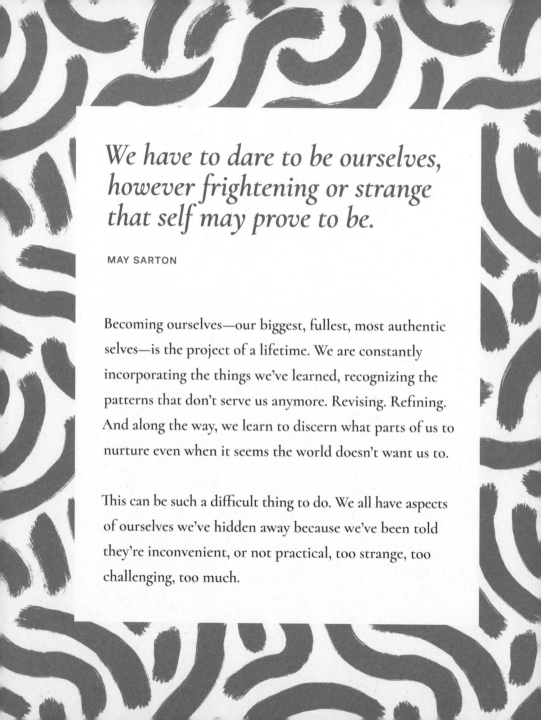

We have to dare to be ourselves, however frightening or strange that self may prove to be.

MAY SARTON

Becoming ourselves—our biggest, fullest, most authentic selves—is the project of a lifetime. We are constantly incorporating the things we've learned, recognizing the patterns that don't serve us anymore. Revising. Refining. And along the way, we learn to discern what parts of us to nurture even when it seems the world doesn't want us to.

This can be such a difficult thing to do. We all have aspects of ourselves we've hidden away because we've been told they're inconvenient, or not practical, too strange, too challenging, too much.

What are some authentic parts of yourself that you tend to "turn off" or "shut down"?

Are there places where you feel more comfortable showing these aspects of you? Or people who help you access these parts of you?

Imagine making a gentle commitment to yourself: a commitment to embody these elements of yourself more regularly. What are three small but important ways to give these parts of yourself room to be?

I'm trying to find
my own version of
what makes me feel
beautiful.

TRACEE ELLIS ROSS

From unrealistic images of bodies and faces to impossible portrayals of how we should look as we age, our society has so many ways of making us feel we don't measure up.

We might feel like "too much" in some respects, and in other respects, "not enough."

The messages can be so consistent, so overwhelming, and so convincing that it can be difficult to remind ourselves that there is nothing wrong with our bodies. One of the best ways to bolster ourselves against these messages is to remember and affirm—over and over again—our own versions of beauty.

What are the garments or rituals, places or activities that help you see, feel, and acknowledge your own unique kind of beauty? Do you feel beautiful while making a meal? Beautiful while weeding the garden in your oldest jeans? Beautiful with the windows down on the highway and singing? The things that make you feel beautiful don't have to make sense to anyone else. This is a place to note and celebrate them for yourself:

EVERYTHING SEEMED POSSIBLE, WHEN I LOOKED THROUGH THE EYES OF A CHILD. EVERY ONCE IN A WHILE, I REMEMBER: I STILL HAVE THE CHANCE TO BE THAT WILD.

Nikki Rowe

TAKE GOOD CARE

When you were a child, what did you imagine your grown-up life would be? What promises did you make yourself? That you'd have ice cream every night? That you'd always walk around barefoot? That you'd stay up until midnight reading? What do you think the child you were would say about the adult you've grown up to be?

Adult responsibilities are real, and the truth is that we can't always be as wild and carefree as our younger selves might have suspected we'd be. But it's also true that there is probably a lot more potential for childlike joy in our lives than we're currently accessing. What are a few suggestions your younger self wants to offer you?

My younger self is probably a little surprised I don't:

My younger self would want me to remember:

My younger self thinks I should have more:

Boundaries teach people how to treat you, and they teach you how to respect yourself.

CHERYL STRAYED

Even if the concept of setting boundaries is new to you, it's likely you've done some of this work in your life already. Even if you weren't thinking of them as boundaries, you've laid down some ground rules in relationships with loved ones, friends, and coworkers. You may have stated these boundaries out loud, or you may have been less direct—but either way, people in your life have at least some idea of the kinds of actions and behaviors you won't accept.

What are some boundaries you've communicated verbally?

What are some boundaries you've communicated nonverbally or indirectly?

Be careful how you
talk to yourself because
you are listening.

LISA M. HAYES

Think about the inner voice you use—the kinds of things you say in your own head, *to* yourself and *about* yourself every day. When you make a mistake, do you treat yourself with understanding? Or are you hard on yourself instead? Do you give yourself credit for the work that you've done and the things you achieve? Or do you tend to focus on the tasks you haven't yet finished, the things you haven't done perfectly?

Before you answer the questions below, take a day to pay close attention to the way you speak to yourself—the kinds of things you may not have even noticed you say.

When are the times you tend to speak to yourself with understanding and flexibility?

When are the times you tend to speak to yourself harshly?

How might you interrupt your own patterns of self-criticism?

Love yourself enough to set boundaries. Your time and energy are precious.

ANNA TAYLOR

If you're used to giving a lot, the idea of giving less may feel challenging. But chances are there are at least a few places in your life where you're giving more than you're truly comfortable with. Are you responding to nonurgent work emails on the weekend? Do you stay late, do you arrive early, do you have a habit of being the most generous, most helpful friend?

What are the places where your tendency is to prioritize others at the cost of your own well-being?

What are three areas where you'd like to dial back how much you give? These could be specific places, projects, or relationships.

What are three concrete ways, no matter how big or small, you'd like to offer less?

Remember what 'yes' feels like.

OPRAH WINFREY

Yes and no aren't always as clear and obvious as we think. When we're trying to find our answer in the mix of our opinions, other people's opinions, our responsibilities, and our histories, getting a clear yes or no is often confusing. Calibrating what yes and no feel like for you individually can be powerfully clarifying.

Think about people you love, things you love, situations where you have been *glad* to say yes. Think about the word itself. *Yes.*

What does this feel like in your body? What sensations move through you? What happens to your energy level?

Think now about challenging situations, things you do not like, moments when you know deeply that your answer is no. Think about the word *no.*

What does this feel like in your body? What sensations move through you? What happens to your energy level?

This yes/no calibration can become a tool for you whenever you need to clear away some background noise and figure out for yourself what it is you want, what your true preference is, what you actually need.

I'M A RECOVERING PERFECTIONIST,
AND AN ASPIRING 'GOOD ENOUGH-IST.'

Brené Brown

Where does perfectionism show up for you?

Do you believe you have to be the perfect employee, the perfect host, the perfect guest, the perfect child, the perfect partner, the perfect friend? Are there specific ways you hold yourself to an impossible standard?

When you think about setting aside perfection for "good enough," what do you imagine you might lose?

What do you imagine you might gain?

What are three specific things you want to aspire to be "good enough" at, rather than perfect?

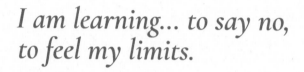

I am learning... to say no, to feel my limits.

ADRIENNE MAREE BROWN

"I'll be there on Saturday," "I'm happy to volunteer," "I can bake a batch of cookies."

How many times lately have you said yes to something before giving yourself a chance to think?

If you have a tendency to give without considering your own needs, give yourself this challenge: pause before agreeing to things. It could be five minutes or it could be a few days, but make it a new habit to wait for a moment before you commit to giving your time and energy away.

Your partner, your sibling, your boss... who do you tend to immediately say yes to?

"I'll need some time to get back to you." "I'll have to check my calendar first." What's a go-to statement you'd like to create to make sure you give yourself time to consider?

"Thank you for thinking of me, but I have to say no," "I appreciate the offer, but I don't have the time." What are some phrases you want to have handy in the future when you say no to something?

I am tired of being brave.

ANNE SEXTON

So many of us have a tendency to downplay the difficulties in our own lives. To be strong for longer than we truly have energy for...

We make ourselves be braver than we want to be.

And while this can be useful from time to time, making this a daily habit is exhausting.

When someone you love tells you that they're tired of something, chances are you believe them. Take this moment to offer yourself the same kindness—acknowledging your limits with honesty and authenticity.

What's something you're truly tired of being?

What are some ways and places this fatigue tends to show up?

If you imagine an alternative way of being, what does it look like?

...you can slow down...

You're enough.

You've always been enough.

DR. THEMA BRYANT

Do you have a habit of over-extending yourself, working until you're exhausted, and *then* giving yourself a chance to rest? If you have a tendency to live at top speed, it can be helpful to notice the patterns—when does this happen? *How can you notice the signs that your energy is running low, and restore yourself before your well runs dry?*

Make a simple promise to yourself...

The next time I feel myself:

...I will slow down by:

There are a thousand reasons
to live this life...

MARILYNNE ROBINSON

On the good days, it's easy to remember the bright things—
the things that comfort us, please us, amaze us, sustain us. They're as small
as clean sheets or as big as a promotion. As simple as a favorite breakfast,
or as complex as a dear friend who offers us exactly the right kind of
affirmation.

But on the difficult days, those things can feel like they belong to a different world altogether, a different self, a different life. This page is a place to collect as many of those delights as you can.

This page is a library of reasons to love this life.

They'll be here so you can revisit them whenever you need. As often as you like.

Care for your *boundaries*

IT IS LIBERATING... TO NO LONGER HIDE WHO WE ARE.

Dr. Jean Cheng

Hiding ourselves can be more subtle than it sounds.
It can look like staying quiet about a preference, diminishing an aspect of your personality, trying not to rock the boat, avoiding disagreeing in order to keep the peace. It can be subtle enough that it's hard to notice, or it can be all-encompassing.

Are there any relationships, places, or communities in your life that require you to hide an aspect of yourself?

What do you think might happen if you showed those hidden aspects of yourself?

Imagine yourself... inside the protective eggshell of your own imagined boundary.

KARLA MCLAREN

Imagine, even on the tumultuous days, a portable sense of calm and peace—a way to access stillness, groundedness, and ease. With a little bit of visualization and practice, you can create your own sense of sanctuary. And the more you work with accessing it, the easier it will be.

Imagine a space that extends around you on all sides and above your head, as far as your arms can reach. Think of it like a little, private room you can pop up around yourself during a challenging meeting, in stressful rush-hour traffic, or when you feel overwhelmed by someone else's energy.

What are some qualities of this space? Is it solid? Is it porous?
Is it made of light?

How do you feel while you're inside it?

What does it offer you protection from?

When are some moments when accessing this space will be
particularly useful to you?

I believe in me
more than anything
in this world.

WILMA RUDOLPH

Deep beneath any self-doubt or questioning, there's something else—a part of you that's solid and clear on what you are capable of. A part of you that believes in you, quite deeply. A part of you that's unshakable in what it knows to be true. It may be strong and well-rooted, or it may be as small as a seed, but it's real and it has a lot to say, if you give it space to speak.

Without overthinking, try to access that sense of confidence. Let it fill in the answers below, without censoring or second-guessing. *What does that part have to say to the rest of you?*

One of your truest gifts is:

You have a rare and remarkable ability to:

It's time to believe in your:

...I want to remind you what an honor it is for the people who love you to get to meet your needs when they can. *It is a gift.*

LISA OLIVERA

There are so many reasons we don't ask for the things we want and need—we don't want to ask for too much, we don't want to burden the people we love, we're afraid to seem demanding, or we're just so used to handling everything by ourselves.

But something we may be overlooking is the fact that the people who are closest to us might actually *want* to help...

They might actually appreciate the chance to show up for us, and give what they can. And when we can be very open and clear about what it is that we need, we make it easy for others to know whether or not they can meet that request.

Think of three people who are close to you. Is there something you'd like to ask each one for? It could be a simple thing or a more profound change to your relationship or shared ways of being.

Person:

Request:

Person:

Request:

Person:

Request:

I WILL HONOR MYSELF BY BEING BRAVE ENOUGH TO BE DISLIKED. I AM NOT FOR EVERYONE, EVEN IF I'M AMAZING. EVERYONE IS NOT FOR ME.

In a world that asks us to be many things, it can be easy to shape ourselves to fit the room, the relationship, the community, the job. It can be easy to downplay certain parts of ourselves in order to do what we're asked to do, and be who we're asked to be. And while this can be a good and necessary compromise, it sometimes means we are leaving some of the best elements of ourselves behind. What parts of you are you tired of downplaying? What parts of you are you ready to inhabit more completely?

At work, I'm less _____ than I truly am. I'd like to show more of my authentic _____

In significant relationships, I'm less _____ than I want to be. I'd like to access _____ more fully.

On a daily basis, I'd like to practice being myself by _____

Not everyone and everything deserves access to you. Protect your spirit.

UNKNOWN

Friends, families, organizations, communities... it's likely that there are a lot of individuals and groups that want access to your time, your talents, and your energy. It's wonderful to be wanted and needed. But it's also important to notice when the relationship is all one-sided, disrespectful, or has developed patterns you find damaging.

Is there anyone in your life who often leaves you feeling unsettled, uncertain, or confused?

What are the things they do that tend to impact you in these ways?

How can you protect yourself or offer less energy to this relationship?

Be ruthless for your
own well-being.

HOLLY BUTCHER

So many of us are raised to put others first. To meet the needs of the room instead of our own. To ignore our own preferences in service of someone else. Along the way, we start to lose sight of what we would prefer.

If the word "ruthless" in the quote on the opposite page was especially surprising for you, this might be particularly challenging and necessary work to do. If you're someone who would never dream of being ruthless, explore this concept for a moment. This isn't a suggestion to go about hurting people's feelings for no reason, but it is an invitation to explore the places and ways where being a little more self-serving might support your own sense of well-being.

If no one's feelings would be hurt, I'd:

If I didn't care what anyone thought, I'd:

If people didn't expect me to do it, I'd stop:

Do these answers point you in the direction of some changes you want to make for your own well-being and health?

...keep telling yourself that you're allowed. You're allowed to leave.

ERYNN BROOK

Permission to mute, permission to block, permission to unfollow, permission to get off the phone, permission to end a conversation, permission to leave... this is a reminder that you should always have these things. And it's a reminder to notice when some part of you is asking to go... and to take that part of yourself seriously.

The process of reminding yourself that you can leave is the process of acknowledging your own discomfort, prioritizing your feelings, and recognizing that those feelings have something to tell you.

And you can start small—with identifying what your experience has been or tends to be. Understanding how the feeling of wanting to leave shows up for you can help you understand it more quickly when it shows up in the future, and can help you be clearer on what you want to do.

These are the physical sensations I often get when I want to leave:

This is an account I'd like to mute or unfollow, or a digital space I might want to leave:

This is a situation or physical space I often feel I want to leave:

When it comes to leaving something, I want to remember to trust my:

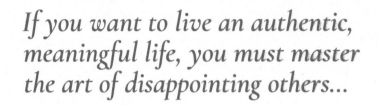

If you want to live an authentic, meaningful life, you must master the art of disappointing others...

CHERYL RICHARDSON

In order to avoid disappointing others, we disappoint ourselves instead. Maybe, if it's become a habit, we disappoint ourselves dozens of times a day, constantly ignoring what we want in small (or big) but meaningful ways. We text back even though we're honestly too tired, we say yes to the date we know we don't want, or we go along with a friend's dinner suggestion instead of the dinner we'd prefer. We settle for our second choice, or for not even getting the thing we want at all. "I don't mind," we say. "It's no trouble to me." But your inner self feels differently.

Your challenge is to find a small but authentic way to disappoint someone else (instead of yourself) five times this week. If you think these kinds of situations will be hard to find, you're about to be surprised! The intention is not to disappoint someone for disappointment's sake—it's to disappoint someone in the service of being authentic to your own needs and preferences. (And, of course, this isn't an appropriate exercise to use with people whose health, livelihood, or well-being depend on you.)

---

(1) Who I disappointed:

How it felt:

(2) Who I disappointed:

How it felt:

(3) Who I disappointed:

How it felt:

(4) Who I disappointed:

How it felt:

(5) Who I disappointed:

How it felt:

Did disappointing others feel different over time? How was the experience of this week for you?

I don't have to explain why I need a break. Not even to myself. I do not have to earn rest.

YASMINE CHEYENNE

Do you have a habit of rushing from one thing to the next? Do you feel guilty when you take a break, unproductive for pausing, or like you're slacking off if you need to rest? What if you offered yourself at least one break for recalibration every day? If you're someone who identifies a lot with productivity, it can be especially helpful to do this in a spontaneous way—not as a reward for finishing a project, but simply because it's something you're ready for. Simply because it's something you need.

Recalibration can be whatever you want it to be—a cup of tea, a snack, a few quick text messages to someone you love, some mindful stretching and breathing, a two-song dance party. It's a way to tap into some rest, some joy, or some connection. It's a way to remind yourself that the most important thing in your life isn't productivity.

Write as many options for recalibration as you can think of in the space below, so you can come back to them whenever you need.

Whatever I'm doing,
I'm in that moment
and doing it.

SADE ADU

We multitask for so many reasons—because we're moving so quickly, because there's so much to do, because we're overwhelmed and feel like we need to be managing everything.

Even in the midst of the most hectic day, there can be a surprising amount of self-care and generosity in allowing yourself to do just one thing.

Just one errand, one project, one task from start to finish. You might even feel your inner swirl of thoughts calm down. You might find that your brain or body or spirit really appreciates working like this.

When does multitasking tend to show up for you?

What are a few projects, tasks, or activities you'd like to try doing by themselves, without the distraction of anything else?

YOU HAVE TO FEEL. IT IS THE REASON YOU ARE HERE ON EARTH. YOU ARE HERE TO RISK YOUR HEART.

Louise Erdrich

The pace of our current world often serves as a distraction. Slowing ourselves down and quieting our minds is something we tend to resist because we know that if we do, we may find ourselves face-to-face with a difficult emotion. In the short term, it seems easier to keep ourselves busy with something else. But in the long term, we know that those difficult emotions don't just go away. They don't heal or transform until we've acknowledged them, heard them out.

You don't have to give yourself over to challenging feelings all day every day. But giving them a little space to present themselves can be profoundly healing.

It's revealing to open the door to the feeling that's been knocking and hear what it has to say.

This is a place to do that work. You can set a timer if you like—just two minutes or five or seven. You can thank this emotion and then let it know that you need to move on with your day. (You may wish to do this exercise with more than one emotion or feeling!)

I haven't fully explored it, but I think this feeling is bigger than I've acknowledged:

It's here because:

It wants me to know:

Perhaps the most healing
words you could say...
I love all of you.

YASMIN MOGAHED

For many of us, it's much easier to imagine loving all of someone else than it is to imagine loving all of our own selves. But what if you started here and now? What if you chose to commit to loving just one part of yourself you've always thought of as difficult—treating that one part with exceptional kindness, softening the way you think of it?

This is something about myself I find difficult to love:

This is how I feel when I see that same quality in someone else:

One small step toward loving and accepting this quality in myself would be:

In the future, when I think about this quality, I'd like to remember that:

Care for your
possibilities

YOUR BOUNDARIES CAN CHANGE AS YOU GROW AND CHANGE...

TAKE GOOD CARE

Your boundaries don't live in one place forever. And they don't stay the same. Your boundaries are a function of you, which means that as you change, they change.

It can take some paying attention to realize that a boundary needs to move. And once you realize it does, you get to decide what that means—whether you want to change your own actions, make new decisions, or share these changes with the people you're close to.

This is something I'm getting more at ease with:

This is something I'm getting less at ease with:

This is a way of being that suits me less than it used to:

This is a new way of being that I feel drawn toward lately:

Sometimes we need to create boundaries with ourselves as well, because we need to unlearn old habits.

LATHAM THOMAS

Boundaries aren't just a tool to use in service of healthy relationships with others; they're also a tool to use in service of healthy relationships with ourselves. Boundaries with ourselves are a way to act in our own best interest, in alignment with our values, and for our own well-being. A boundary with yourself could mean sticking to a budget, not eating foods you're sensitive to, turning off your phone at a certain time each night, or reading before bed instead of scrolling social media. Any boundary you set for yourself is intended to help you care for yourself better.

What are some self-boundaries you already have—boundaries you
do well at sticking to?

What are some self-boundaries you'd like to implement, or boundaries
you'd like to stick to more predictably?

What are you clearing space for?
What are you tending to?

CHANI NICHOLAS

Creating new limits in our lives isn't just a way to shut down behaviors and situations that don't work for us; it's also a way to create new space for the things we want, the hopes we have, the ideas we want to take seriously.

Think about the limits you've set, whether old or new...

What parts of you do they protect?

What do they make room for?

What future dreams are they in service to?

Your worth is not measured by your *productivity.*

UNKNOWN

Often, the messaging we get from the world asks us to measure our value by the things we're accomplishing. If we aren't careful, we start to think of a "good day" as a day in which we got lots of things done, and we start to see ourselves as "worthy" only when we're working hard.

But there are so many other ways to frame the idea of what makes a day good. What if a valuable day is one in which you allow yourself to rest? What if the best use of an afternoon is disconnecting, or creating, trying something new, lying on a blanket in the park?

What if "productivity" meant tending to your self...

your mind, your body, your well-being, your health? Not in the name of getting more done tomorrow, but simply because you deserve to experience contentment and joy.

How many different ways can you finish the following statements?

A good day can be one that's in service to my:

A day can be worthwhile if all I do is:

Instead of productivity, I want to think about my days in terms of:

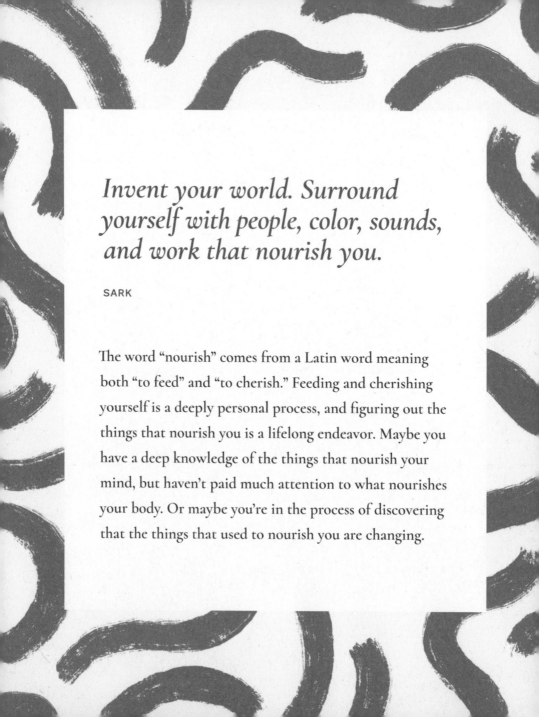

Invent your world. Surround yourself with people, color, sounds, and work that nourish you.

SARK

The word "nourish" comes from a Latin word meaning both "to feed" and "to cherish." Feeding and cherishing yourself is a deeply personal process, and figuring out the things that nourish you is a lifelong endeavor. Maybe you have a deep knowledge of the things that nourish your mind, but haven't paid much attention to what nourishes your body. Or maybe you're in the process of discovering that the things that used to nourish you are changing.

These are my favorite foods and habits for nourishing my body:

These are ways I love to nourish my mind:

These are the ways I nourish my spirit:

What would it look like to care for your mind, body, and spirit more fully?

...IT'S OKAY TO SAY, "YES I AM GOOD AT THIS..."

Simone Biles

So often, we're taught not to brag, taught not to shine "too brightly," or call too much attention to ourselves. We learn to emphasize modesty. It's why we tend to deflect a compliment rather than receive it fully. It keeps our spirits smaller than they want to be.

There's nothing wrong with being good at something.
There's nothing wrong with acknowledging this. Every single one
of us deserves to stand in the light of the talents we have and feel
good about it.

This is a place to note everything you're good at. Unabashedly.
Fill out every single one of these lines, and then... find another
piece of paper. Add to it often. Keep going.

I am good enough, worthy enough, and important enough to demand more.

CHIDERA EGGERUE

If you have a lot of practice in being accommodating, advocating for yourself by asking for more may be unfamiliar. Asking for more doesn't mean you aren't grateful for what you already have. But it does mean you're speaking up for your own wants and needs. And it means you take your own self-worth seriously.

If demanding more feels challenging, start small. Start with close friends. Start with people and situations that will support you in this work you're doing.

When are some moments in the past when your requests for more of something have been met?

What's something you feel ready to ask for more of in the near future?

What's a long-range list of tangible or intangible things you'd eventually like to have more of in your life?

Ask for what you want
and be prepared to get it.

MAYA ANGELOU

How clear are you on the things you truly want?

Do you have a hazy idea, a general sense, or can you name, see, and describe them in detail, clearly?

Having a clear picture of the things you want *doesn't* always mean that you'll get them, exactly as you want them. But it *does* offer you a map of the territory, which means that you get a lot of clarity around whether you're moving closer, going in the right direction, and making choices in service of your dream.

What's something you're wishing and working for?

Describe it in as much detail as you can—what it looks like or feels like, its characteristics, how it would be to have access to it.

Even if you aren't in control of the outcome, what's one thing you're doing to bring you closer to this?

I am no longer accepting
the things I cannot change.
I am changing the things
I cannot accept.

ANGELA DAVIS

TAKE GOOD CARE

In order to identify that something in your life needs to change, the first step is acknowledging what doesn't feel right. Before you can build a new boundary, it's helpful to know what work you want that boundary to do—and why you want it to exist.

What are the things in your life you cannot accept? Maybe some of those things are so tiny they feel silly listing. Maybe some of them are so big they feel daunting. But write them down here. Let this be a list of things that do not work, things you no longer want to live with. Underline the ones that you feel ready to explore changing.

I don't want to be a passenger in my own life.

DIANE ACKERMAN

We aren't in control of everything. There are situations that are out of our hands, and things we can't change. But there are also places where we're in the passenger seat, waiting instead of steering. Sometimes all we need is a gentle reminder that we can take the wheel whenever we'd like—whenever we're ready. Whenever the moment is right.

What's an area of your life where you've been riding along instead of driving?

What would taking the wheel look like for you? Is this something you feel ready to do?

There are more valuable things in life than safety and comfort. Learn. *You owe it to yourself.*

NNEDI OKORAFOR

By the time you reach a certain point in your life, it's likely that you've stopped being a beginner at things. When we receive so much positive reinforcement for what we're good at, it can start to feel uncomfortable to begin again.

But there's joy in new things. There's joy in not knowing, and joy in discovering.

Deep down, are there things you want to explore? Things you've been drawn to for as long as you can remember, things you've always wanted to try?

I am willing to risk being bad at:

I am willing to be a beginner at:

I have always wanted to try:

WE... NEED TO KEEP GROWING EVERY MOMENT
OF EVERY DAY THAT WE ARE ON THIS EARTH.

Ruth Asawa

You aren't who you used to be. You are still becoming.
Your growth may not always be clear to you, but if you look back,
you can see it. This is a place to honor your effort and yourself.
This is a place to give yourself credit.

Five years ago, I was:

Since then, I've made so much progress in:

Even in the last year, I've:

Just this week, I've been making progress in:

Push yourself a little
further than you dare.

AUDRE LORDE

There's territory beyond the limits of your every day.
If "as far as I dare" is a fence you've built for yourself, what lies
beyond it? What if you cut a little hole in that fence? And then,
what if you climbed through it?

What are three ways or places that going a little further than
you dare appeals to you?

What stories or beliefs keep you from trying?

If you could commit to exploring just one of these, what would it be?

What motto or mantra do you want to create for yourself,
as you commit to this act of daring?

COMPENDIUM.
live inspired

Written by: M.H. Clark
Designed by: Jessica Phoenix
Edited by: Bailey Vega and Amelia Riedler

ISBN: 978-1-970147-85-8

1st printing. Printed in China with soy and metallic inks on FSC®-Mix certified paper.

Create meaningful moments with gifts that inspire.

CONNECT WITH US
live-inspired.com | sayhello@compendiuminc.com

   @compendiumliveinspired
#compendiumliveinspired